First published in 2010
by Franklin Watts

Copyright © Franklin Watts 2010

Franklin Watts
338 Euston Road
London NW1 3BH

Franklin Watts Australia
Level 17/207 Kent Street
Sydney, NSW 2000

To William and the one thing of all we grew that
you would eat

Series editor: Sarah Peutrill
Art director: Jonathan Hair
Design: Jane Hawkins
Photography: Victoria Coombs/Ecoscene (unless otherwise credited)

Credits: Ricardo A Alves/Shutterstock: front cover t. R Carner/Shutterstock: 12b. Chepko Danil/istockphoto: 17b. Digital Skillet/istockphoto: front cover bc, 22br. Kim Gunkel/istockphoto: 6b. Ideeone/istockphoto: front cover b. Magdalena Kucova/istockphoto: 6t. Robyn Mackenzie/istockphoto: 27b. Nikonov/Shutterstock: 7c. Penny Oakley: title page, 13b, 22bl, 23b. Achim Prill/istockphoto: 21bl. Ravenestling/istockphoto: 8br. Dale Robins/istockphoto: 21r. Kim Pin Tan/Shutterstock: 10t. Arnaud Weisser/istockphoto: 7b.

Every attempt has been made to clear copyright. Should there be any inadvertent omission please apply to the publisher for rectification.

Thanks to Jasmine Clarke and Tony Field, seasoned gardeners, for kindly sharing their gardening knowledge.

Dewey number: 634.7'5

ISBN 978 0 7496 9297 1

Printed in China

Franklin Watts is a division of Hachette Children's Books,
an Hachette UK company.
www.hachette.co.uk

Safety notice:

Gardening is fun! There are a few basic rules you should always follow, however. Always garden with an adult; any pesticides and fertilisers should be handled by adults only and applied to specified plants only; wear appropriate clothing and footwear and always wash your hands when you have finished in the garden.

Grow your own
Strawberries

Helen Lanz

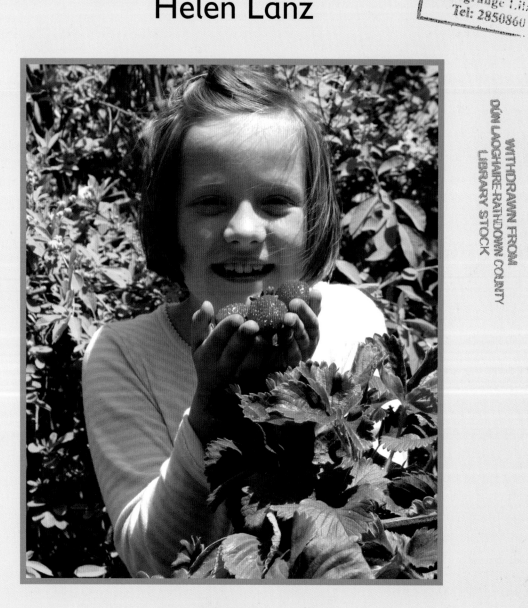

W
FRANKLIN WATTS
LONDON•SYDNEY

Contents

Words in **bold** are in the glossary on page 29.

Why grow your own strawberries?

When you think of summer, what do you think of? Sunny days, being by the sea, eating ice cream? What about eating strawberries? In summertime, there is so much lovely fruit to eat, including blueberries, raspberries and delicious, sweet strawberries.

Freshness and flavour

How about growing your own strawberries? Homegrown strawberries often have a lot more flavour and you can't beat them for freshness.

◄ Strawberries are easy to grow at home.

You don't need a garden!

You don't need a lot of space to grow your own strawberries. They are happy to grow in pots and containers.

Better all round

It's fun to grow your own, and you can be outside a lot and get some exercise. But it's not just good for us, it's also good for our **environment**, too. If we only have to step into the garden or go to a windowsill to get our fresh fruit and vegetables, we don't use petrol to travel to the shops to fetch them.

▲ A healthy strawberry plant will have shiny, dark green leaves.

Flower

Leaf

Crown

Roots

SCIENCE SPOT

Close-up of a strawberry plant

The roots of a strawberry plant grow from the **crown**. This is why it is important to plant them carefully, making sure the crown is just above the soil, but not too **exposed**.

7

Be prepared!

So, you've decided to grow some strawberries! Before you get going, it's a good idea to prepare what you will need.

All about you...

You will be outside a lot, so you will need some old clothes that your grown-up helper doesn't mind if you get dirty. Don't forget about your feet – wellies or old trainers will do.

◀ Gardening gloves, a trowel and small fork may be useful, but not essential.

▶ You will need a watering can (or you could use a jug).

… and your strawberries

You can grow strawberries in most types of large container.

If you do grow them in a pot, rather than in a vegetable plot, you will need some soil. It is a good idea to add **compost** to a pot or plot.

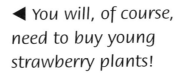

▲ Your strawberry plants will look attractive popping out through the holes.

◄ You will, of course, need to buy young strawberry plants!

▶ It is important to feed your plants to help them to produce fruit.

Top tip!

Keep a growing diary, writing down everything, from the strawberry type to how and when you did things. This will help if you decide to do it again, and will be fun to look back on. If you have a camera, you could take pictures as well.

Plants or seeds?

You might be surprised to learn that it is usual to grow strawberries from plants, rather than seeds.

Top tip!

Leave buying your strawberry plants until you are ready to plant them outside. It is best to plant them out straight away.

◀ You can buy strawberry plants from your local garden centre.

▲ Strawberries are unusual because their seeds are on the outside of the fruit.

SCIENCE SPOT *Seeds*

Seeds contain all the ingredients needed to grow into adult plants. A seed can wait until the **conditions** are right for it to **germinate**, or start to grow. It usually needs to be dark, damp and wet.

Growing from seed

You can try growing strawberries from seed, but it can be tricky. If you do have a go, you will have to wait for a year to see any fruit.

Before the growing season (see page 28) thinly sprinkle the seeds over damp soil in seed pots or a tray. Place in a sunny, warm spot on a windowsill. When seedlings are 10cm tall, **transplant** them into bigger pots.

As the weather grows warmer, get the young plants used to being outside (see panel), before planting them out in pots or 25cm apart in the ground. The plants should fruit the year after you plant them out.

▲ Follow the seed packet instructions when sowing your seeds.

Hardening off

If you have grown your seedlings yourself inside, it is a good idea to get them used to being outside before you plant them out. To do this, place the seedling pots outside during the day, bringing them in at night. Do this for a couple of days. This is called 'hardening off'.

Pot or plot?

Strawberries love warm, sunny spots, with plenty of direct sunlight and no shady bits – and they do like to be sheltered from the wind.

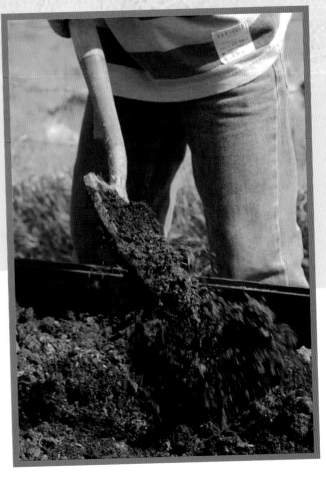

▲ Make sure you have dug the soil well before planting.

They don't need much room – they can grow in a plot or in a pot.

Preparing a plot

Strawberries like well-prepared soil, so dig it well and add lots of compost. As you prepare the bed, remove any weeds.

Preparing a pot

You can grow strawberries in the specially-shaped strawberry pots, which have cup-shaped holes for each strawberry plant. However, they grow just as well in normal, large plant pots.

▶ Specialist strawberry pots look attractive, but your plants will grow in any container.

Put broken pottery or large stones into the bottom of your pot to help with **drainage**. Then add soil and compost until the pot is almost full. If your pots aren't too big, move them about your garden so your plants are always in the sun.

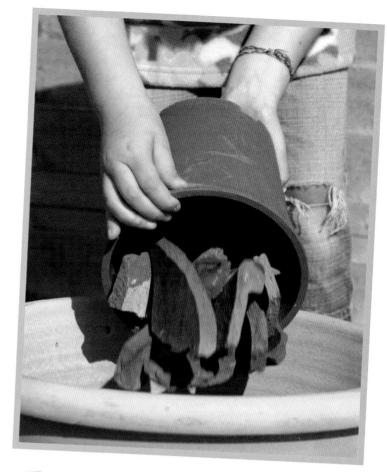

▶Broken bits of pot help with drainage.

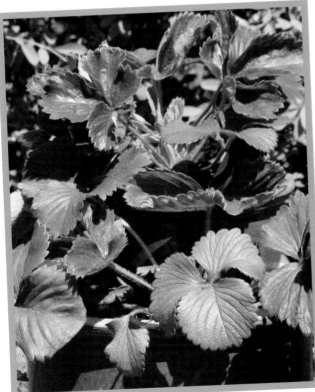

▲ The strawberries will cascade down both pots as they grow.

A strawberry cascade

You can create your own **cascading** strawberry 'fountain'! Be sure to position your pots before you fill them. Use a very large plant pot on the bottom, add broken pottery pieces for drainage and fill with compost and soil. Place a smaller pot on top, towards the back of the large pot, leaving enough room to plant strawberry plants at the front of the large pot. Fill the top pot as normal.

Planting out

▲ *For smaller pots, plant just one strawberry plant. Bigger pots will take more plants.*

Did you know that there are many different **varieties** of strawberry (see page 26)? If you choose a summer-fruiting variety, you should get fruit about two months after planting.

Planting out

Plant out your new strawberry plants on the day you get them (as long as it's the right time of year to plant out – see page 28). Check the plant label for details of your chosen variety.

SCIENCE SPOT *What it takes to grow*

Your strawberry plant will need sunlight, water and **nutrients** to grow. Although soil isn't always necessary for a plant to grow, it does hold the nutrients and water that a plant needs and gives the plant support to stay upright. A plant's leaves are the really clever part. They use sunlight, water and the gas **carbon dioxide** to make a store of energy to help the plant to grow.

Step-by-step

1. Take the young plants out of their pots and soak their root balls in water for about an hour.

2. Dig a hole in your soil and place your strawberry plant in it. Make sure the crown of the plant (see page 7) is just above the soil line.

3. Gently, but firmly, press the soil around the base of the plant.

4. For a plot, plant the young plants about 35–40cm apart. If you have more than one row, make sure your rows are about 90cm apart.

5. For a pot, place one strawberry plant per cup or hole, or two plants per normal (large) pot.

6. Now all that's needed is a well-deserved drink – don't forget to give your plants one, too!

Tending the crop

Strawberry plants have **shallow** roots. This makes them good to grow in pots, but also means you need to water them regularly, especially in hot weather. However, take care not to overwater your plants as they don't like soggy roots!

▲ Poke your fingers into the soil to check that it's damp underneath. If the soil sticks to your fingers, the plant does not need more water yet.

Helping the roots

Take off the first flowers to make sure the plant focuses on growing strong. This helps to get a good root system.

When the plants have become strong, ask your grown-up helper to start adding a liquid **fertiliser**.

▲ Only remove the early flowers. It is the flowers that eventually form the fruits.

◄ Ask your grown-up helper to add the fertiliser to your plants' water once a week.

Runners

Your plants may produce '**runners**' a month or so after planting. Take these off so they don't take energy away from your plant producing fruit.

▶ A runner is a shoot that comes from the main plant and develops into a new plant (see also page 25).

Runner

(see also page 25).

Pollination

SCIENCE SPOT

Many plants rely on insects to carry the male **pollen grain** to reach an **ovum**, or egg, in a female plant of the same plant family. The pollen grain must reach the egg in order to **fertilise** it and grow fruit. Strawberry plants can self-pollinate – the pollen in a flower can fertilise an egg in the same flower.

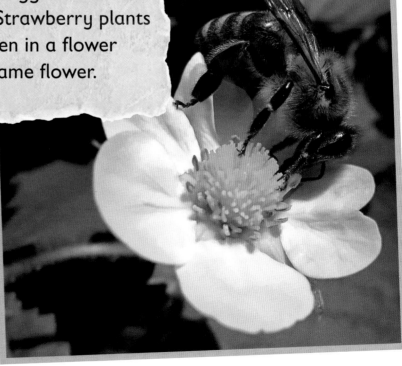

▶ It is not necessary for a bee to pollinate a strawberry plant, but a bee travelling from plant to plant does make sure the flowers are pollinated evenly and the strawberries fully form.

Take good care

To keep your plants healthy you need to weed between them – this helps to protect your plants and fruit from **disease**.

Good watering

Keep checking that the soil does not dry out. Make sure you water at the crown of the plant and try not to wet any fruit as it may make them rot.

▶ *Try to water at the crown of the plant.*

Top tip!

Top tip!

For strawberries planted in beds, it helps to cover the soil with straw just before, or as fruit starts to appear. This stops the fruit from lying on the ground and getting diseases or rotting.

18

The first fruit!

Keep checking your plants – you will soon see some tiny green strawberries appear. Soon the green strawberries will grow and ripen in the sun and turn into red jewels!

▶ *Water, plant food and sunshine help the fruits to grow plump and ripen to red.*

Stop the birds!

Be careful, the garden birds are watching, too! You will need to keep birds off your ripening crop. Putting **mesh** over your plants is one way to keep them safe.

◀ *You could also use the free CDs that sometimes come with newspapers as bird scarers.*

Pests and diseases!

Sometimes **pests** and diseases can cause problems. The best way to avoid them is by checking your crop often. This way, you will notice if there are any problems and stop them before they get too bad.

▲ Clear away rotten leaves and weeds from around the bottom of your plants. This helps to prevent diseases.

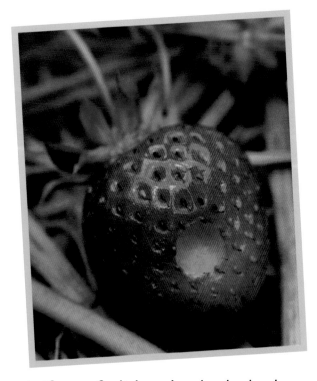

▲ If your fruit is going bad, check if you need to put down straw; if you are splashing the fruit when watering or whether birds have pecked at it (pictured).

Frost

Cold and **frosts** can damage your strawberry plant's flowers. If a flower has opened and goes brown in the middle because of the frost, it is unlikely it will fruit. Protect your plant by covering with straw or scrunched up newspaper.

Wet

Strawberry plants don't like to get too wet. Fruit will rot if left to rest on soil.

Aphids

Hungry **aphids** can destroy your plants. One way to get rid of these pests is to gently brush them off with a soft paintbrush or old toothbrush. Do this as soon as you see them and keep it up until they don't return. You can also try gently washing them off with used washing-up water.

Some aphids carry diseases as well. If this happens, get rid of the infected plant so it doesn't affect your other ones.

► Aphids cling to plant stems and suck the sap, or juice, from the plant. This photo shows them much bigger than in real life.

▲ Keep a look out for slugs! They can be yellow, brown or black.

Slugs

Slugs like to eat strawberries as much as the birds. Try to put them off by laying grit or broken egg shells around the base of your plants.

Harvest!

Are those berries looking red, ripe and ready to eat? Yes? Well, they are ready to harvest.

Reaping the rewards

Congratulations! This is the bit that you've been waiting for. All your hard work is about to pay off! Now it is time to pick your own bowlful of strawberries.

▶ Be sure to pick any ripe strawberries quickly so they don't rot on the plant.

Delicious!

All you need to do now is give your ripe strawberries a good wash in cold water and pull or cut off the green stalk.

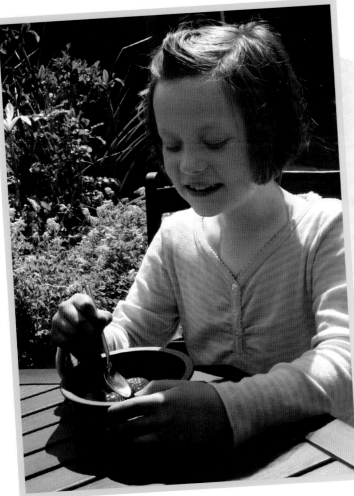

SCIENCE SPOT *Power food*

Strawberries are not only delicious, but they are very good for you. They contain lots of **vitamin** C. This helps your body repair itself and keeps you strong enough to fight off coughs and colds.

What next?

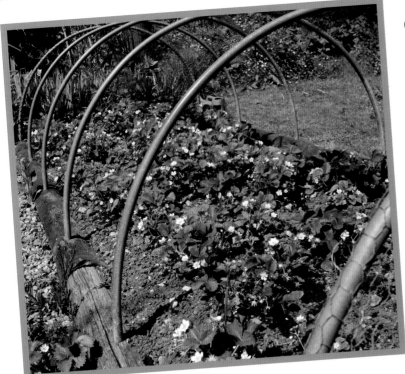

Once you've harvested this year's crop of strawberries, don't just abandon your strawberry plants. They will come back year after year.

◀ *Strawberry plants will probably give you a good crop for five or six years before you need to replace them with new plants.*

Overwintering

Strawberry plants are quite **hardy** so are usually fine to be left outside over winter. However, you will need to clear away the straw at the end of the growing season. Pull off any dead leaves so the plants are left uncluttered and healthy to face the winter.

◀ *A sharp frost in the crown of a strawberry plant, out of season, can often help it produce a good crop of fruit the next year.*

Propagating

During the growing season, a strawberry plant will produce 'runners'. These are baby or 'daughter' plants that shoot out from the main plant. You can use these runners to grow new plants for next year.

Step-by-step

1. Fill a pot with soil and allow the runner to root in this pot while still attached to the main plant.

2. After a month or so, when the runner is well established, you can separate it from the main plant and pot properly. This is called propagating – or breeding from another plant.

3. If your main plant throws out more than two runners, remove these otherwise the main plant will weaken, leading to a poor crop of strawberries.

Super strawberries

Strawberries are delicious eaten on their own or with cream or ice cream. There are hundreds of recipes you can use them in too. There's one here, but you could search the Internet for more.

◀ There are lots of delicious recipes you can make with strawberries.

Strawberry varieties

There are three summer-fruiting types of strawberry: early, mid and late plants, all producing fruit early- to mid-summer. There are also **perpetual** fruiting strawberries, which produce fruit throughout the summer and into autumn. There are many varieties within each group.

◀ Alpine strawberries are tiny and full of flavour – they are great for making jam.

Strawberry cheesecake

Ask an adult to help you with the chopping and cooking.

Ingredients

Base
- 250g digestive biscuits
- 100g melted butter

Filling
- 600g cream cheese
- 100g icing sugar
- 300ml whipping cream

Topping
- 25g icing sugar
- 400g fresh strawberries (sliced)

Method

1. To make the base: melt the butter in a saucepan. Place the biscuits in a plastic food bag and crush with a rolling pin. Tip the crumbs into a bowl and pour over the melted butter. Mix well. Tip the mixture into a greased 23cm, loose-bottomed tin and press down firmly. Place in the fridge to chill and set for one hour.

2. To make the filling: put the cream cheese and icing sugar into a bowl. Beat with an electric mixer until smooth. Pour in the cream and continue to beat until all the ingredients are mixed well. Now completely cover the biscuit base with the cream mixture. Leave to set in the fridge overnight or for a few hours.

3. Topping: remove the cheesecake from the tin and place on a plate. Place the sliced strawberries on top. Sieve the remaining icing sugar over the top.

Your pudding is ready to serve! Tell everyone it's made with homegrown strawberries!

Gardening calendar

Here's an 'at-a-glance' guide to the growing year. Planting and growing times vary, depending on where you live, but you can follow these general guidelines.

Early winter (Dec–Jan)
Weed around strawberry plants.

Late winter (Jan–Feb)
Think about any new varieties to plant. If using seeds, sow them now.

Early spring (March–April)
Give established strawberry plants some liquid fertiliser.
Prepare pots or plot for any new plants.

Late spring (April–May)
Plant out early-bearing strawberry plants at the beginning of this period; place under **cloches** if still frosty. Plant out mid- and late-bearing strawberry plants towards the middle of this period.

Lift cloches on sunny days to allow pollination. Look out for runners. Place straw under developing strawberries. Water plants well. Protect berries from birds.

Early summer (June–July)
Place straw under developing strawberries; water plants well. Protect berries from birds. If propagating early runners, cut from main plant.

Early fruits ready to harvest at the beginning of this period.

Late summer (July–Aug)
Keep plants well watered. If propagating mid and late runners, cut from the main plant.

Mid and late season fruits ready to harvest. Perpetual varieties ready to harvest towards end of this period.

Early autumn (Sept–Oct)
Give early, mid and late varieties a boost by cutting back and feeding with fertiliser.

Perpetual varieties ready to harvest at beginning of this period.

Late autumn (Oct–Nov)
Give perpetual varieties a boost by cutting back and feeding with fertiliser.

Gardening glossary

aphid: a small plant-sucking insect.

carbon dioxide: a gas that is part of the air around us.

cascading: a mass of something falling or hanging.

cloche: a plastic tunnel that protects plants from the cold.

compost: a mixture of soil and rotting plants used to fertilise, or feed, plants to help them grow.

conditions: the situation or surroundings that affect something.

crown: the strawberry crown grows at the soil line. The leaves and buds of the small fruit begin here. The crown stores food for the plant and provides support for it.

disease: an illness.

drainage: in this case, to allow water to flow through the soil and leave the plant pot or bag, to stop the soil from becoming too waterlogged leading to rot.

environment: the area in which something exists or lives and also the whole of the natural world – the skies, seas, lands, plants and animals.

exposed: open to the air and weather.

fertilise: to make the soil better for growing plants by adding nutrients.

fertiliser: a substance such as manure or a chemical mixture used to make soil more fertile.

frost: frozen water droplets that freeze on the ground on cold mornings.

germinate: the process when seeds sprout and begin to grow.

hardy: able to survive under poor or extreme weather.

mesh: netting, often made from light plastic, to stop pests.

nutrients: something that gives goodness and nourishment needed for growing or being healthy.

ovum: the female part of the plant.

perpetual: never-ending.

pests: insects or animals that are destructive to a plant, such as slugs.

pollen grain: a fine powder which is produced in the male parts of a plant.

runners: a shoot that comes from the 'mother' or main plant which can be grown into a new plant.

shallow: not deep.

transplant: to remove from one position and replant somewhere else to continue growing.

varieties: different types of the same plant family.

vitamin: a key nutrient that the body needs in small amounts to grow and stay strong.

Index

Useful websites

www.bbc.co.uk/gardening/gardening_with_children/

www.gardeningwithchildren.co.uk
Gardening activities and information about how plants grow.

www.rhs.org.uk/schoolgardening
Find out about school gardening projects and clubs or play the gardening game.

www.rhs.org.uk/growyour own/strawberry.asp
Advice on growing strawberries, including varieties.

Gardening club

Have you enjoyed growing your own? How about joining a gardening club? Your school may have one. You could grow fruit and vegetables which could be cooked and eaten as part of your school meals and snacks, or make ladybird homes to help attract them to your garden. If your school doesn't have a gardening club, why not talk to your teacher about setting one up?

Note to parents and teachers: Every effort has been made by the Publishers to ensure that these websites are suitable for children, that they are of the highest educational value, and that they contain no inappropriate or offensive material. However, because of the nature of the Internet, it is impossible to guarantee that the contents of these sites will not be altered. We strongly advise that Internet access is supervised by a responsible adult.